The Proper Care and Feeding of Church Volunteers

A Practical Guide for Volunteer Leaders

Gary A. Petri

Sheed & Ward
Kansas City

Sheed & Ward™ is a service of The National Catholic Reporter Publishing Company.
ISBN: 1-55612-916-5

Published by: Sheed & Ward
115 E. Armour Blvd.
P.O. Box 419492
Kansas City, MO 64141-6492

To order, call: (800) 333-7373

Illustrated by Michelle E. Petri.

Contents

Acknowledgments

Special thanks to my daughter Michelle, who created the cartoon characters used in the book, and my wife Barbara, who edited the many revisions of this work.

Others who should receive recognition are Father Gerry Gonderinger (St. Stephen the Martyr Church, Omaha) and Father Michael Grewe (Holy Ghost Church, Omaha) for their expertise and encouragement. Also, Nancy Teply of Bergan Mercy Medical Center in Omaha, who shared her insight into hospital volunteers and Dan Knobbe of St. Patricks Church, Elkhorn, Nebraska for help in understanding the volunteers who work with youth.

Foreword

Vatican II has been called the Council of the Laity and the Decree on the Apostolate of the Laity sets forth very clearly that it is the responsibility of all the people of God to be involved and penetrate the world with the Spirit of Christ. It challenges the members of the Church to permeate the world with the Spirit of Christ. God's people, by reason of their baptism and confirmation, are all called to share the mission of Christ. The American bishops in a pastoral document entitled "Called and Gifted" emphasized this vocation of the laity to share in the sanctifying work of the Church. In 1995, fifteen years later, the Bishops in a new statement refocused this message and applied it to the Third Millennium. Our Holy Father has called for renewed efforts in evangelization as we approach the year 2000, so the importance and urgency of this involvement becomes quite obvious.

We thank God that the laity does respond, for without the many volunteers found in all our parishes and in Diocesan ministries, we could never rise to this challenge.

The author of this short little book tells us how we can best find, train and make the most effective use of these generous parishioners. This very practical "how to" book should be very helpful to pastors and lay leaders as they make sure their volunteers are well-equipped to carry out and fulfill the ministries in which they are involved. The very prudent and practical suggestions in this text, along with the forms and attachments in the back of the book, provide great help to any coordinators of parish programs, whether these coordinators are new to the ministry or have been involved for some time. The author has been working very diligently in the ministry of evangelization and offers this help out of his long experience. I am sure that his suggestions will be of value to all our parish leaders who at this time are intensifying their programs in preparation for the new millennium. The Church is to be a sign of God's kingdom in the world, a task turned over by Christ to us in the power of the Holy Spirit. We must equip our people who offer to share this trust. This little book can prevent us from making any serious mistakes and should help us all to build up God's kingdom among us.

Most Reverend Daniel E. Sheehan
Archbishop Emeritus
Archdiocese of Omaha

ONE

Why on Earth?

Yes, that's a very good question. What's the big deal? Isn't it expected that devout churchgoers volunteer their time to various projects? Why on earth do we need a book that talks about church volunteers?

In order to answer this, one need only go to a religious bookstore and spend some time looking at the titles on various types of church volunteer work. Most of these are in the area of "ministry," and they all seem to focus on the "how-to's" of that specific function, e.g., lector, usher, stewardship, etc. Nowhere do you find instructions on how to select, manage and motivate volunteers . . . let alone on how to handle any of the many sticky situations that often arise when dealing with this unique group.

The practical suggestions offered in this book can be of use to anyone from the pastor, secretary or other members of the staff, to the choir director or head usher. Anyone who finds him- or herself responsible for one of the multitude of organizations or ministries in the church could find this work helpful.

My own personal motivation for writing this book comes out of years of experience of being on the "other end of the stick," if you will. We can all remember times when someone else was in charge and, unfortunately, didn't have a clue as to how to treat volunteers. We might have been misplaced in our volunteer jobs because our talents were not a good match with the ministry. We may have been given too much to do or too little time to do it. Or maybe we didn't receive adequate instruction or training. We might have found ourselves suffering from burn-out or frustration caused by lack of recognition. Whatever the situation, we can all remember when being a volunteer was not all that much fun. In fact, we may have felt tempted to "chuck the whole thing."

From my limited search of the materials available, there doesn't seem to be much out there to help a ministry head deal with these kinds of problems. If we look across the aisle into the business or management section of the bookstore, we can find volumes on management styles, motivation and supervisory techniques. Unfortunately, working with volunteers is just different enough from the business environment to make applying these business practices a little dangerous, at least without some careful study and modification. Even for paid positions, the church is not known for its outstanding monetary reward/recognition systems.

A friend of mine once commented that "if the church was a business, it would have gone broke around the year 73 AD." We can joke about the lack of help in this important area and the obvious need for it, but we also have to remember the continued working of the Holy Spirit. This wonderful gift and presence among us keeps us moving forward. We have all heard the expression "the church succeeds in spite of itself."

We all have good and bad experiences that we can share. Sometimes we can learn more from a bad example than we can from a good one. This book is an attempt to share my experience of being a volunteer and my observations of successes and failures of people who work with volunteers.

The bad news is: there is no easy way to learn the technique of managing a volunteer group. Reading and studying is a good beginning, but this must be followed by practice in the real world. Success seems to require an alertness to the situations around us and a desire to learn from each experience. By that I mean that every encounter with a volunteer needs to be prepared for before hand and evaluated after the fact. We need to determine if there was some way to improve the contact. Did this encounter encourage the volunteer to continue in the ministry . . . and did the person feel better about their investment of time? Sure, this is an ideal and it won't happen every time, but we need to aim for that goal.

TWO

Why Me, Lord?

Volunteers are extremely important to the church. In fact, it is safe to say that the success of the church is due in no small part to volunteers. These are the folks who do the multitude of thankless jobs that make up the everyday operation of the church. The church couldn't function without them.

If this is true, it is hard to understand anyone having an attitude that sees volunteers as mere things to be taken for granted, like cogs in a wheel. One member of the clergy was heard saying that it was no big deal if "John" didn't work out in this volunteer job because "we can always get someone else." This attitude assumes there is an endless supply of people all lined up waiting to take a turn under the church's yoke. After all, that's what's expected of us. It's something similar to the old description of the laity's duties to "pray, pay and obey," except that it leaves out the fourth element, "expect to volunteer for whatever is needed in the church." Well, that doesn't cut it anymore.

With Vatican II, the laity (who after all make up the vast majority of volunteers in the church today) have become aware of their real importance in the church and the dignity that goes along with it. People rightly expect to be treated like the valued assets they really are. If they are not, the church's teaching is meaningless in the real life they experience.

Anyway, part of being a volunteer is the mysterious way we end up being involved in this or that particular thing. A few were "called to service" by a sudden blinding thunderbolt and trumpet's blare, like St. Paul. But the majority "fell into" their niche through what can be called more normal circumstances. These are the folks who decided to help because nobody else would do the job. Or maybe they were asked in such a way that refusing would call down the wrath of God on them and their descendants for a thousand generations. In this respect, some church leaders could give lessons on the art of guilt. Then there are the others who just happened to be in the wrong place at the wrong time like poor Simon of Cyrene. Sometimes you want to stop, look up to heaven, and ask, "Why me, Lord?"

Whatever the "call," we volunteers all find ourselves in the service of the church. Underlying this should be the "spirituality of the volunteer." In other words, regardless of how we get the call, we volunteers would do well to see God's providential hand in the circumstances that led up to this point. For some reason we have been seen in this particular service by God from all eternity. What a profound thought. God must think so much of us and the talents He has given us that He wants us to be active ministers in His Body, the church. Let's not get all hung up in the technical definition of minister/ministry. If we view the various volunteer functions within the church, we see that they can all be viewed as ministry. The person, should therefore, have "an attitude of service."

The volunteer has been elevated by God to a part-time service of His church. If we believe in our theology, this means that the person can expect specific graces to help him or her perform that function. What a marvelous gift from God! It is only in heaven that we will fully understand and appreciate these magnificent blessings that daily come to us from our Heavenly Father.

Along with having this attitude of service, the volunteer should see prayer as a vital part of what he or she does – prayer for those they come in contact with, prayer for others in their group who share their ministry and prayer so that they can know the will of God and carry it out for His honor and glory.

This attitude of service and the development of the spirituality of the volunteer is as important in the big picture as the end goal or work of the ministry itself. We don't have greeters at church to simply open and close the doors for people on Sunday. They shine forth the welcoming presence of God and the whole community to the visitor. They become a symbol and a sign of God's presence to those who come to worship. If this isn't the case, we would be better off installing automatic door openers like the grocery stores.

This is probably the one area that is often overlooked in dealing with volunteers. We are so goal oriented and we can get so focused on the "task at hand" that we completely neglect the spiritual formation of those involved in the group. We'll return to this subject in more detail in a later section.

THREE

Lazarus, Come Forth!

The image of Jesus calling Lazarus might be a bit dramatic, but we can find it useful as we turn our attention to those who have responsibility to lead a ministry or organization. One of the perennial problems in a volunteer work force is the recruitment and selection of new and re-placement members. Calling people forth to use their talents in a lively fashion brings us right back to the image of Lazarus.

From now on, we will focus our attention on the volunteer leader. In the business world we might use terms like supervisor or manager. In the church world, these words are far too threatening because they conjure up images of boss-worker or supervisor-subordinate relation-ship. The volunteer world prefers gentle terms like "coordinator" or "contact person." That's O.K., as long as we know that many of the functions this coordinator will be doing closely resemble the job duties of a supervisor or manager in the business world. We'll see this in more detail later.

There are a few general comments that should be pointed out without further ado:

1. We can't really identify all the various problems facing a volunteer coordinator, let alone solve them. At best, we can expose a few of the most common situations and establish a few common sense principles. We can then apply these general approaches on a case-by-case basis. Sure, you can call that a first class cop-out.

2. The involvement of the registered members of the church commu-nity in various organizations and ministries is absolutely essential to the survival of the church and the continued spiritual growth of each member. Studies have repeatedly shown that members who are involved in activities beyond Sunday worship services

develop an attitude of "ownership of the church." Because of this, they stand a much better chance of surviving the tough times that face all of us at one time or another in our faith journey.

3. When selecting or recruiting volunteers for any particular organization or group, prayer is essential: prayer before you begin the selection process, during the process and after the conclusion. This may seem unnecessary to mention in a church environment, but many times we can get so caught up in the immediate battles, we forget Whose banner we are fighting under. Now, having said that, we can proceed further into the area of recruitment and volunteer selection.

Casual observation tells us that there is a world of difference between finding volunteers in a brand new parish versus an older, established church. Lets look at the dynamics of each situation.

In a new parish there might be just a few groups existing and many organizations and ministries are competing for volunteers. Because of the newness, the individual talents of people are really not known. On the other hand, newness brings a certain excitement and enthusiasm that makes recruitment in a young parish easier than in an older community.

The older parish usually has many existing ministries and organizations. Some have outlived their usefulness but continue to exist because people are afraid to pull the plug. Others have members and leadership that have become stagnant through the years and, as a result, resist any sort of change. The existence of cliques might also present additional problems. The list goes on and on. In the older parish, the primary recruitment concern centers around the replacement of volunteers who move on to other activities.

Let's take a moment and look at several recruiting methods. The first, and maybe the easiest, is what we could call the "broadcast method." Here the requirements of membership do not demand specific talents, skills or experience. The Sunday bulletin is the usual vehicle used for this method. We have all seen notices asking for volunteers to clean the church, bake a cake or whatever. Almost anyone can respond and help according to their time and abilities. However, this is not a good approach if the project or group requires more specific talents. An example might be the search for a new member of the finance committee or for a new organist. Skills and talents of a definite nature are required to successfully function in these specialized areas. Here again we notice similarities with the business world.

The second recruiting method we can call the "individual invitation." Here we are looking for possible candidates who possess something specific that we have targeted. As an example, people who are outgoing and friendly would be good candidates for greeters. People with business or finance background might be candidates for openings on the finance committee. Other examples might immediately come to mind.

The advantage of this method is the selectivity you have in controlling who is considered a candidate. However, this requires a list of possible volunteers. Now, where does this list come from? You might remember the words attributed to St. Ignatius of Loyola: pray as if everything depended on God, but work as if everything depended on you."

If you are new and don't know the people well enough personally to develop a list, several possible solutions come to mind. The Pastor and the parish staff can be a valuable source of contacts. Usually in a medium to large size parish, there are a few "insiders" who are known to be both level headed and discrete. These folks can also assist you with the names of a few possible candidates. Of course, first-hand knowledge and experience of people and their talents is best.

Another approach uses the "search committee" to develop a list of possible candidates. This method can be used to fill openings on the parish council or a school board. The key, of course, is to have members of the search committee who know many people in the parish and can avoid perpetuating something like the "old boy's club."

There are other opportunities for recruitment that must be a part of any successful volunteer coordinator's bag of tricks. One is the "special event" like a Ministry Fair or Sign-up Sunday, which is part of any good Stewardship Program. The other opportunity comes at registration time, when each family gives its vital church statistics. Registration in the parish can be used to "probe interests" in various ministries and organizations. Let's look at both of these.

The special event is becoming more popular as parishes gain experience with the stewardship of time and talent. Some of the most successful events combine the actual sign-up process with something fun and exciting like an ice cream social or pancake breakfast. Anything can be used to entice people into attending. Imagination is the operative word here. You also need to take a tip from the business world and make sure that whatever you do is done well. When you ask people to become a part of a group, that first image is so very important. Handouts with mission statements and current goals of the organization are a great way to let people know what the group is all about. They also show that thought and planning played a big part in this function. A professional-looking card or tent sign naming the organization says as much about the group as the mission statement. Anyone with a PC and a decent printer can generate these.

The time of registration can be a "golden opportunity" if used to your advantage. In many parishes, people are allowed to register on the fly, as it were. They catch the Pastor after services, and he hands them the registration form with the hurried instructions that they should fill it out and drop it in the mail or bring it by next Sunday. And your opportunity goes out the door with them.

Some parishes have successfully started a more formal registration approach. You can't just grab a form and rush out the door. Either the Pastor or someone from the parish staff will visit with these newcomers. This gives the parish leadership the opportunity to make sure all the blanks have legible answers on them, and also to extend a more personal welcome to the newcomers. Now, here comes the pitch. What better time to talk about the various ministries and organizations in the parish than when these folks are sitting in the parish offices relaxing with a cup of coffee? After all, these folks are new and they just might have questions that you can answer for them. At the same time, you have the opportunity to assess their interest in the various groups. Any registration form worth its salt should also have volunteer opportunities listed along with the usual name, address, and sacramental information (Sorry for the editorial comment). Attachment 1 is an example of such a form.

Before we leave this subject, we need to mention a few other common-sense items. The first is the importance of contacting a person who has just volunteered for a ministry or organization. So many people have been hurt by being ignored or neglected after they raised their hand and offered their time and talent to a church group. It seems that they have "fallen through the cracks." If someone volunteers – at registration time, at a special event or whatever – make sure the ministry head contacts that person ASAP. This contact should (1) thank the new volunteer for offering to join the group, (2) reinforce the group's need for their particular talents, and (3) officially welcome them aboard. What kind of a message do we send when someone volunteers and we ignore them? More than likely, we will never see that person raise their hand again. Mishandling like this can account for many who have even left the church. Of course, we also want to schedule the new volunteer into a particular ministry or activity as soon as possible. Training might be required, so every effort should be made to provide this in a timely fashion.

If we firmly believe that a parish's vitality is in direct proportion to the involvement of its members, it makes sense that we actively pursue them and invite them to become active. This becomes a ministry of itself – an outreach to the "registered inactive."

There are two approaches to consider. One utilizes a telephone solicitation approach, and the other, a letter of invitation. Both assume the parish has sufficient computer capability to run a simple sort and match of ministry/organization members against the church registry. The result is a list of registered members who are not yet involved. This also assumes the parish database has current and accurate information on those who are active.

Attachment 2 is an example of a telephone script that can be used to contact these inactive members. The calling volunteers should be selected for their outgoing and friendly manner as well as maturity and discretion. The results of these contacts must be recorded properly but should also be treated in strictest confidence. Training and role-play are important parts of building up the confidence of these telephone volunteers. Let's face it, this is tough duty – but one that can pay great dividends. Attachment 3 is an example of a letter of invitation. The intent is to make this gentle, yet persuasive. The letter can be even more effective if it is followed by a phone call.

A special plug should also be made for periodic homilies that invite each parishioner to participate in at least one parish ministry or organization. It is difficult to sell this philosophy unless it is supported and encouraged "from the top."

This is such an important area in the managing of volunteer groups that it forms the foundation for almost everything that is said beyond this point. Once we have identified and selected new volunteers, we need to focus our attention on training.

FOUR

You Should Have Told Me!

One common area of frustration for new volunteers is the lack of training. They may have been given a task that they have little background in, or they may not have a clear understanding of exactly what they are expected to do and how it fits into the "big picture." If you have never had this happen . . . consider yourself lucky!

Now, let's get serious. When we talk about volunteer training, we are not talking about a big hairy deal. A new volunteer needs to know a few very basic things that will insure a successful project completion.

Another point to keep in mind is that each volunteer group is just a little different in the "technical" training it should receive, i.e. Eucharistic Ministers, Lectors, Musicians, etc. We need to view several aspects of volunteer training.

First, volunteers need to learn some general background about the group they belong to, what's expected of each member (attendance at meetings, etc.) and what the goals and objectives are for this particular group. It might also be helpful to explain how this group contributes toward the overall goal of the parish as stated in the mission statement. This goes a long way in letting the new volunteer feel that he or she is making a valuable contribution to the entire parish and not just one little segment. Another element of this general training should allow the new volunteer an opportunity to meet the other members of the group. This makes the person feel "connected" and also makes it easier to find a substitute in the case of an emergency or a conflict in scheduling.

The technical portion of the training deals with the specifics of the particular ministry or organization. These instructions are the "how-tos" of that group. We all make our share of mistakes in life, but to send a new volunteer out without any instruction is just increasing the chances for mistakes and a sense of frustration on the part of the volunteer.

There are a number of excellent works on the market that describe specific ministries, such as Lectors, Ushers, Eucharistic Ministers, etc. Using these as the core of the technical training, you only need to supplement them with your "local customs." These include the mundane items like where the keys are kept, how to set up for the service, what do you do with the collection after the Offertory, etc. These little details are sometimes very important, especially if the new volunteer has not paid close attention to these functions before they joined the group.

Now let's talk about the person who does the training. If you are the volunteer coordinator in a particular ministry, you ultimately have the responsibility to provide your people with adequate training. This can be done in any number of ways, however. You can do it yourself, if you're an extrovert and love speaking before a captive audience. If not, you'll need to find another approach.

Many parishes have training packages already developed for the various ministries. Some have even gone so far as to capture a training session on video for use in later sessions. If this doesn't exist in your parish, you might check with neighboring parishes. Some Dioceses have staff members who will train new volunteers in these various ministries. Another valuable source might be the Deacon community. Often these dedicated folks make themselves available for presenting these types of training sessions. Of course, your other option is to enlist the services of another member of the group who is outgoing, experienced and willing to conduct the sessions.

No matter how the training is given, your presence as the coordinator is important. You will become the volunteer's point of contact for questions and they will look to you for leadership.

Before we leave this topic, we need to conclude with something dramatic. No, we're not talking about fireworks or party hats – we're talking about some ceremony for the new volunteers following the training. They need a blessing or some equivalent that "commissions them" to now officially act in their ministry or group on behalf of the entire parish.

This ceremony may be simple or elaborate. The "commission" may be done immediately after the training, or it may be done at the conclusion of a Sunday Service. Some parishes "commission" the entire group (both new and old volunteers) for the coming year, e.g., Religious Education Teachers and Assistants. Whatever the case, this little ceremony should be meaningful for the group. Attachment 4 is an example of such a service that takes place outside the Eucharist. Attachment 5 is another example of a blessing for Catechists that takes place within the Mass. There are several resources available that contain a collection of these ceremonies.

Also, something tangible like a medal or holy card could be given to each participant. This way they have something to remember the occasion. Psychologically, this ceremony is important because the new volunteers sense they have been given the power to function in their new role. If there are other parishioners present, as would happen at a ceremony after Mass, they would add their affirmation to the event.

Now that we have recruited and trained the volunteers, we need to focus our attention on the proper supervision of these wonderful people.

FIVE

Get Off My Back!

If you've never had a boss who hovers over you and drives you crazy, consider yourself very lucky. Supervisors seem to fall into two categories: those who smother you, and those who ignore you. Isn't there something in between?

Whether you like the term or not, supervision is exactly what you are doing if you are a "contact person" or "coordinator" of a group of volunteers. In the church world, we don't like the words supervise or manage . . . after all, those are business terms and we are talking about volunteers. But when we look carefully, we see that in both the business and church worlds, the goal is a superior end product. Our motivation may (or should) be different, but we are both striving for a finished product that is of top quality.

Let's face it, as a volunteer coordinator, you are responsible for the recruitment, selection, training, motivation and, sometimes, the correction of volunteers. Don't these sound like functions performed by a supervisor or manager in the business world? The real secret to what you do is *how do you do all this without getting under everyone's skin?*

We have all probably heard the clever saying about a business needing only three things for success: "location, location and location." Well, in supervising volunteers, we could change the wording a little and say "communication, communication and communication." This seems so simple that many people might be tempted to forget this wisdom. We can look around us and see examples of a lack of communication where the coordinator is "just too busy" to pass the word along, or the sad case of a program director who might feel a certain sense of power because he or she has more information than the others in the group. Whatever the case, the result can easily be hurt feelings and misdirected energies. Let's look at some specifics of communication.

We're going to assume that the coordinator is familiar with the importance of eye contact, body language, voice tone, etc. These are the basic mechanical skills of communication. Instead, let's pursue the question of what to communicate. The first point that comes to mind is to communicate the goals of the group and the individual work assignments. All members of the group must work together to assure a successful completion of the goals. The importance of clear instructions can't be overemphasized. So many projects have been "botched up" because one person, through no fault of her own, got the wrong idea from the coordinator. I read once that the supervisor needs to give instructions in the simplest terms he or she can. It's far more important for the supervisor to transmit information in a clear, simple fashion than to impress the listener with his or her splendid vocabulary and higher level of learning.

In the process of communicating work assignments, there seem to be three basic elements that need to be covered: the "what," "who" and "when" of the task. *What* is the exact description of the work activity the volunteer is expected to accomplish? *Who* is the responsible party – this individual alone, or as part of a team, and who are the other team members? The *when* describes the deadline for completing this task. In the process of communicating, if you detect some hesitation on the part of the listener, make sure that there is a clear understanding of these three elements before the encounter is complete. Some people feel embarrassed about asking questions, so you need to read between the lines and be looking for warning signs so you can "head this problem off at the pass." There is nothing wrong with the coordinator taking the initiative and asking, "Is everything perfectly clear?" Or maybe, "I may not have explained this very well, so shall we go over the details again?" Taking a little extra time to clearly communicate the instructions when assignments are made can really help the success rate of any project.

A rather obvious comment can be made here about decision making. Just because you were elected, appointed or just fell into the leadership role, you really don't share any Papal Infallibility. A consensus form of management and decision making is very appropriate for volunteer groups. Many times you can learn new approaches from others in the group. Remember the old saying, "Two heads are better than one." Some groups are run like a Middle Age fiefdom or a dictatorship. Collaboration and respect go a long way.

Another sensitive area for the supervisor or volunteer coordinator is follow-up. We are all anxious for the project to succeed, and some tasks require "touching base" with the responsible person so that we know how things are going and if additional help may be required. This can be done either by the direct or indirect method. The direct approach is to ask the person directly about his or her progress. The indirect approach is more subtle and relies on information "once removed." You can learn valuable progress information by listening to others who are working with the individual. So many functions are interrelated that often we don't even have to ask the responsible person how things are going. This information is volunteered by others. In either approach, there is a careful balance that must be kept in order to avoid becoming a "hoverer." No one likes a supervisor who constantly demands progress reports. The poor worker feels that he or she spends more time reporting the progress than actually doing the work.

The only way to learn this balancing act is by trial and error. It also depends somewhat on the person being supervised. Some volunteers may require closer contact than others. Experience with people is a valuable asset in this department. One person may enjoy reporting progress while others might feel this is an intrusion of privacy. The key factor is to know your people and determine the best way to keep in touch without bothering them.

On a philosophical note, by selecting, training and commissioning volunteers, we have given them the power to act, which also implies the power to fail. We are all driven toward the goal of perfection in what we do; however, some don't share this passion with the same intensity that we do. Sometimes failure can be good. If used properly, failure can teach valuable lessons that can never be learned by an easy success.

Now let's look at the important issue of motivation. In church work, the prime motivator should be the greater honor and glory of God. Nobody in his right mind works for the church for purely monetary considerations. However, if you know of someone like this, please suggest professional help! Having said that, we need to remember what many saints have said or written about motivation. These insightful people have observed and commented that even the holiest of intentions are always "tainted with earthly motives." Holiness consists in the struggle to focus our motivation on pleasing God. It sure sounds easy.

Following this observation, if we look at a typical church volunteer, we will find a "mixed bag" of motives. There may be 56% glory of God, 27% glory of self, 15% fear of going to hell, and 2% undecided. It helps if we keep this in mind when we supervise volunteers. We need to encourage the growth of the "higher motives" through the use of spiritual foundation tools. What John the Baptist said seems right on target, "He must increase while I must decrease" (John 3:30). We will see more about this a little later. For the present, let us look at some techniques for motivation on the purely human level. No matter who we are or where we are in our spiritual journey, we all are human and have some basic human needs that should be addressed.

Since we can't very well use annual appraisals, salary treatment or bonus pay as a motivator, it seems that the primary tool for volunteers becomes "feedback." We have talked about keeping in touch with our volunteers on the progress of their work efforts. This is an ideal time to give them some feedback on how they are doing. Encouraging them with positive comments is called positive reinforcement. This tool is used everyday in the business world. Studies have shown that most people respond favorably to positive comments about their efforts. This continues the process of letting the volunteer know she is a valued asset to the church. Her efforts are not in vain, and her work is sincerely appreciated.

Negative feedback can also be effective, but here we need to proceed with caution. Again, supervisors must know their people and how they may respond if confronted with negative criticism. If the volunteer is simply going to be crushed and burst into tears at the slightest comment, you had better search for a different approach. If handled tactfully, most people will accept the feedback for what it is – an honest attempt to help them improve their work. It may help to begin such a discussion by explaining this motive before you get into the details. It is also very effective if you can combine and balance negative comments with positive observations within the same contact. This "takes the edge off" the negative.

We will continue this topic in a later section, but for now, let's agree that volunteers have a right to know how they are doing. This right to know includes both the good and the bad. If we don't face up to this responsibility, we are failing as a supervisor. Part of the respect we owe all volunteers is shown by our willingness to share the truth with them. A compliment is almost always well received. It also helps if we can remember that volunteers are not as delicate as we imagine when it comes to hearing something negative. Again, this area requires careful planning and practice with reading people and knowing how to deal with them as individuals.

Another form of motivation is the use of some sort of public recognition. We talked about beginning this process as part of their training, i.e., the commissioning ceremony. An official pat on the back given in public can be a great motivator. This can be done at one of the Sunday Liturgies or some other well-attended event. Many parishes have a volunteer appreciation dinner or reception. This can be a very formal affair or a simple potluck dinner. Whatever the case, the clergy and staff should host the event and do everything they can to show their appreciation for the efforts of all the volunteers. Awards can be given, groups recognized, prizes handed out – as long as there is something for everyone. And while we are speaking about this, let's remember that when we make out the invitation list for the event, everyone who has volunteered is included. There is nothing so damaging as a volunteer appreciation party from which someone is inadvertently left out. The key to whatever you do is "first class." You want to direct a loud and clear message to the attendees that they are special people, and you really appreciate all they do for the church. Your imagination can go wild with this. You can decorate, have skits, whatever, as long as the event is fun for everyone.

Before we move on, a word or two should be said about *burnout.* This dread disease afflicts many in church work. If we haven't experienced it ourselves, we probably know of some who have.

Sometimes a volunteer jumps into things with both feet, as they say, but before long, they taper off and withdraw to a minimal level of involvement. The causes can be either internal or external. Circumstances in their life may have changed, e.g., job responsibilities, family commitments, etc. It may be a conflict with someone in their volunteer group. It can also be caused by fatigue brought on by trying to do too much. Some people just can't ever say "no." These are external.

The internal causes are rather elusive little devils. It seems that many folks have a built-in timer that goes off after a certain period of time in any volunteer job. It may be 2 to 5 years, whatever. They simply get bored and want to move on. I confess I suffer from this – my timer is usually set for 3 years.

So, what can we do? Well, the Serenity Prayer really comes in handy here: change what you can change, accept what you can't and pray for the wisdom to know the difference. Certain external things are beyond our control – job responsibilities and family commitments. Other things are partially under our control, but we first need a careful diagnosis of the disease. This can sometimes be difficult. Here again, communication is so very important. Problems like conflicts with other members of the group will be discussed in the next chapter.

What about the clock? Here the supervisor is tested in his or her ability to change work assignments often enough to make the job interesting. Doing new things with different people may lengthen the timer setting. However, don't be surprised if the person eventually decides to move on. That's part of human nature.

The burnout caused by fatigue is one problem we can help. The supervisor should be sensitive and attempt to know each person well enough that they can say "no" for him or her. It is so very easy to keep "piling on" more and more on the good volunteers because they always say "yes" and the work is almost always done on time – until something snaps. Our job is to monitor this: take the pulse, check the temperature and if there is even a hint of the "burnout bug," give the assignment to someone else in the group. Again, we come back to that open and honest communication.

One last thought. Let's call it a reality check. Underlying everything we say or do, we need to keep in mind that these folks that God has given us temporarily are *volunteers*. We can't expect them to perform miracles. They have lives outside the church, and many times this volunteer work isn't even close to the top of their priority list. This is a sobering thought, but one that just may help us through some difficult times.

We all come together with our own life stories and our own problems. We are all at different places along our faith journey. We can imitate our Lord here by accepting people where they are and loving them for who they are, not for what they can do for us.

Now let's look at some really difficult situations.

SIX

What a Pain in the Neck!

There are certain people and their behavior that will just drive you up the wall. You can select and recruit volunteers carefully, train them thoroughly and then *pow*, your carefully planned project is in shambles. What happened?

If you are in the business of supervising a volunteer group, it won't take long before you run into one of these "tough cases." There are probably as many variations of these as there are volunteers, but for our purposes, we have selected a few to illustrate some typical problems. It should also be pointed out that this is by no means a complete collection of problem-solving techniques. These examples of problems and possible solutions are but one approach that has worked. There are many other solutions that might work as well or better. Now, let's look at a few tough cases.

Late or no-shows

These folks are always late. If you schedule a meeting at 7 p.m., they waltz in at 7:15. My sister was like that – she was always late. We loved her dearly but if we wanted to eat at 5, we had to tell her to be there at 4:30. Some people are just like that. No-shows are those who have a real problem keeping appointments. They just don't show up. In functions that are critical, like liturgical ministries, this can be more than just a little inconvenient. What can you do?

The first type (latecomers) can be annoying, but if you once diagnose this behavior, you can work around it. You can make sure they, like my sister, have a "start time" that is just a little ahead of everyone else's scheduled beginning. Another "trick" is to maneuver them into a carpool with punctual people. Peer pressure has been known to help them get on track. The danger with this approach is you may end up having the entire carpool late for your function. Another suggestion is to schedule something fun at the beginning of meetings, that way the person who comes late will miss out.

The second type (no-shows) is a little more serious. If the culprit is a server, for example, some churches have had success using a reward system for perfect or near perfect attendance. This approach has also been known to work for adults. However, some won't respond to this tactic. Here you may have to take a more direct approach.

Be sure to emphasize the importance of fulfilling assigned duties during the volunteer training. Many groups stress the point that each volunteer is responsible for finding a replacement if he is unable to make his appointed assignment. Now, if this has already been covered with all the volunteers, you might approach the individual by asking him a few questions. You could ask if his personal schedule has changed in such a way that he finds it difficult to make his church appointments. This gives him an opportunity to select a better time, e.g., time of service for liturgical ministers. If this doesn't seem to be the problem, you may ask if he understands it is his responsibility to find a replacement and if he has a current listing of the ministry group with names and telephone numbers. A final question might be to ask him if there is something you as the coordinator could do to help him fulfill his assignments.

Now, if you strike out with all these questions and the volunteer persists in his no-show behavior, you may have to point-blank ask him if he wants to continue in this ministry. You may suggest that something less demanding might be better for him at this time. You can again point out the importance of attendance in this ministry and ask him to consider something else.

Busybody

This soul takes delight in keeping up with the latest gossip. She has to know everything about everybody. It may be that she is just a frustrated news columnist, but whatever the case, most of the time this can be harmless. The busybody can be dangerous is she spreads gossip that damages an innocent person's reputation. This behavior can be a waste of valuable time and also jeopardize a project if it has a "short fuse" deadline. What does a person do?

If the behavior is harmless, you may choose to ignore it for the time being. However, if you detect the potential for more serious problems, you may have to step in with corrective action. The first thing, of course, is to be very careful what you say around this person. Some sensitive information has been know to become public knowledge 10 minutes after these busybodies pick up the sound waves. This can be especially critical if the group is working in the church rectory.

A further consideration is confidentiality. In many ministries, this is obviously an absolute necessity. Someone simply can't respect this should be asked to consider another area where his or her talents can be better utilized.

However, if confidentiality is not an issue but you believe the problem is really severe, you might arrange the work assignment in such a way that the person has less chance to hear or spread gossip. Working alone in a separate room really cuts down on this kind of behavior, if you can get away with it. It takes imagination to structure the assignments in this way, however. This can be a true test of the supervisor's ingenuity.

Glory hog

I remember my mother describing a lady who was active in church work in one of the parishes in Denver. This woman was never around when the work was actually being done, but she was always first in line if the Catholic newspaper and photographer happened to be there. These "glory hogs" really love the spotlight, and probably would have made great politicians.

This might seem harmless on the surface. However, if hardworking volunteers are cheated out of the credit they deserve, this can become a real morale buster. One approach is to give this person work assignments in which he is solely responsible for a specific task. This might force him to actually do some work. The person will then be credited for the success or failure of the work he does. This also limits his ability to "horn in" on other volunteers' successes. Another approach for this type of behavior is to make sure *all the volunteers involved* receive the credit they deserve. If pictures are taken and names listed, all should share in the glory. This is part of that positive reinforcement we talked about before.

Compulsive leader

This person feels compelled to share the wealth of her leadership talent with everyone. No matter what the group or task at hand, she has the right answer. Another alias these folks have is "know-it-alls." This can be irritating at best, but it can also stifle genuine contributions by other members of the group. Picture the "normal" volunteer who starts to suggest something in a meeting. The compulsive leader jumps in and takes control of the conversation and monopolizes the discussion. The first volunteer will most likely give up. This behavior requires a strong leader who can keep control of meetings and encourage participation from everyone. It may even require making a rule that limits "time on the floor" during discussion until everyone has had a chance to present his or her ideas.

If this still doesn't work and if you discern a danger of serious disruption in the group, you may have to talk to the individual in private. This is not going to be easy, because many times the person doesn't even know she is verbally bullying others. You might experience some success by asking the person to pay particular attention to the suggestions of others during the next meeting; however, you may have to be more direct and ask her to "tone down" their aggressive participation.

Personality conflicts

Your first inclination to this problem is to let these folks work it out themselves. You may be right and time will usually tell. However, if this problem continues and escalates to the point of global confrontation, you had better step in with some course of action. If two people in your group just can't get along, the most obvious solution is to keep them separated. Zookeepers have known this secret for years. Seriously, you can make use of imaginative scheduling so the paths of these two never cross. You can also make sure that their work assignments are in different locations. Think of the chaos if you asked both of them to work the plant booth together at the parish bazaar. Call 911! Keep them separate whenever possible. If you can't, and if the problem threatens the very fiber of your group, you may have to ask one or the other to consider joining another ministry. Of course, you might want to approach the person you felt was the most flexible.

Crusader

This person is admirable in his dedication to a particular cause. He will swim the widest ocean or climb the highest mountain – no obstacle can stand in his way. Herein lies the problem.

While good intentions are commendable and tenacity is usually a prized virtue, if you are not careful, the crusader can literally tear a volunteer group apart. If he has joined the group with the ulterior motive of "converting the group," watch out! Even if all the others in the group share his particular philosophy, if his "passion" lies outside the mission statement and goals of the organization, you can have a problem. Now, how do we handle this situation?

First, we need to admit that these "crusade issues" can be worthwhile in themselves. It is only when they distract us from our mission that they become a problem. Now having said that, it won't take long to diagnose this behavior. At meetings and gatherings of the group, the crusader will try to guide the focus of attention toward "his issue." In other words, he has his own agenda. It doesn't matter if the subject at hand is planning a potluck dinner – his particular topic is introduced and before you know it, the whole focus has shifted and he is on his "soap box." An even more dangerous situation can arise where one or more group members disagree with his particular stand. You can have open warfare. God save us!

Like other problem areas, open and honest communication is the recommended approach. At the first sign of the crusader behavior, visit with the person privately and make sure he understands the mission statement and goals of the group. You might also admit that his issue is very important but it falls outside the scope of this group. This is another reason why each organization or ministry should have defined mission statements and goals that direct the energies of the group toward a common objective.

If this behavior continues after this initial chat, and in your judgment you feel that allowing it to continue might become a serious problem for the group, you need to take the next step. Again, "straight talk" should be used to let the person know his behavior is distracting the group from working toward its goal. You can again stress the mission of the group and point out where his agenda differs. You might ask him if he thinks he can set aside his particular issue for the good of the group. If he simply can't live with this, then you might suggest he look for another group that is more closely aligned in the area of his interests. This is a difficult situation because you are trying to preserve the integrity of the group without injuring the spirit of the crusader. As in most of these tough cases, prayer before and after is so very important.

Entrenched leader

This person is probably part of the "good old boy (or girl) club." She has been in charge of the group for years. In fact, people can't remember the group without thinking of what's-her-name. In itself, this is not bad. However, in most cases, the entrenched leader surrounds herself with like-minded people, and her legacy continues, ad infinitum. As a result, the group becomes inflexible and resists any hint of change. A dynasty is now in operation. In the world of politics, this is the strongest argument for term limits . . . and the shorter, the better!

Some churches have done just that – they have established something like a term limit. Anyone heading a group or ministry can serve as chairperson for no more than two years, for example. This insures a continuous influx of "new blood" into leadership positions. The downside to this is a lack of continuity. Another mechanism some churches have employed is that the "second-in-command" works with and receives training from the "chief" so that transition is easy and the continuity of programs and goals is insured. The second-in-command automatically becomes the chief after the second year of the term.

There are other ways to insure this natural turnover, but this approach seems to be the least painful. If all groups within the church "play by these rules," no one group is singled out for term limits.

Loose cannon

This behavior is the most severe test of your leadership. Pray that you don't have anyone like this in your group. You can recognize them by the disasters they create. Let's look at just two examples.

The summer is progressing nicely and your CYO or youth sports program seems to be doing well. All of a sudden, you begin to get calls complaining about one of your coaches who lets his temper get the best of him. Not in a little way – oh, no. This person curses the umpire, starts a fistfight with the opposing coach, and throws equipment at his young players. To make matters worse, you check the records and find that something like this happened the last two years.

Then there is the case of the Religious Education Teacher who is reported as saying that abortion is really a woman's choice and the church has no business telling her what she can do with her body. A closer look at the records reveals that it has been alledged that she said Jesus really didn't perform those miracles we read in the Gospel . . . those are just fabrications based on mass hysteria which happened at the time.

Earlier problems now seem like a picnic in the park. How on earth do you handle these problems? When you agreed to head up this group, they never warned you about these folks!

These loose cannons are probably the worst case scenarios you will face as a volunteer coordinator. Up to this point, you have managed to get by using tact and finesse. These usually require the heavy artillery. Straight-up confrontation is probably called for, especially if there is evidence that the people have already been warned about their behavior.

The key here is to make sure that they know this type of behavior is not acceptable for people in their positions. If we could back up in time, one of the easiest steps to take is to define acceptable behavior for church volunteers. This may be a formal written statement that requires all volunteers to act in a manner that demonstrates Christian leadership and values. This document might also list some examples of unacceptable behavior. Certainly in the case of a teacher, upholding and defending the teachings of the church is an absolute requirement for the position. Anyone not willing to accept this "contract" needs to find other avenues of personal fulfillment.

If there is one area where we need to exercise strict precaution, it is with those who are trusted with our young people. Because these little ones are vulnerable to any bad example, those who lead and instruct our youth must be above reproach. Now, having said that, let's return to how we deal with these two problem cases.

If such a "statement of expectations" exists, the coach and the teacher should be confronted with this and asked to explain their behavior. Whatever their reasoning, they need to know that repeated behavior will be grounds for replacing them. If this is the first time they have ever been confronted, you need to make the consequences very clear to them. In business, this is called "straight-talk." These people need to know, without a shadow of a doubt, that this behavior is not acceptable. They also need to know that if they choose to continue in this behavior, they will give up the privilege of being involved in this group and functioning in their current position. In the business world, it is not unusual to reduce this to a written notice and have the supervisor and the employee both sign the document. You may want to consider this approach because it does reinforce the seriousness of the situation.

You may feel that this situation is way beyond your ability to properly handle. That's when you call in the big guns – Father. There is nothing wrong with asking the pastor for help. If you do, make sure you have a complete run-down of all the details so that he knows exactly what the situation is. Even if he agrees to handle the confrontation, you may want to be present for the simple reason that you are still the leader of the group. It also helps to have a third party present to witness what was said and the outcome of the meeting.

On the other hand, there is an argument that favors distancing yourself from this confrontation session. The reasoning here is based on the fear that your effectivness as the group's coordinator may be damaged by your direct involvement. This is a tough decision, and you probably need to take into account your knowledge of the group and any other circumstances that could affect the outcome.

Thank God this last situation is rare. You may never have to deal with anything this serious. However, if you do, consult with your pastor before you try to solve the problem yourself. He may have insights and suggestions that are far more valuable than these brief comments.

SEVEN

But What about Us?

So far we have focused our attention on adult volunteers who work primarily in the church environment. There are others who really don't fit into this mold. Two groups of significant size are the younger folks who are preparing for Confirmation and are required to have "service hours" and the large group of volunteers who help in hospitals. We should spend some time looking into their world since they have a few rather unique problems, (or opportunities, if you're an optimist).

Let's assume the common elements from what we have already seen and spend a little time looking at those things that might be different in dealing with these two groups. Let's begin in the hospital.

Hospital Volunteers

The basic difference between the hospital environment and the church setting is the regimentation and formality that exists in the hospital. Because of the nature of hospital work, rules and regulations are part and parcel of the territory. Various Review Boards and Auditors make this regimentation a daily necessity. We can easily see the effect of this in many areas of volunteer management.

Recruitment is a little different in that the majority of people volunteer as a result of personal invitation from staff members and others who are already volunteers. Some hospitals utilize a periodic mailing to churches and synagogues that ask them to print bulletin announcements recruiting volunteers. Hospitals may also have teens who volunteer to meet the service hour requirements of Confirmation. We'll talk more about this in the section dealing with young volunteers. Another source can be the court-ordered community service folks.

Let's now turn our attention to training for hospital volunteers. To begin the process, many hospitals use an application form that provides an opportunity for the person to select work areas that are interesting to them. Usually, the next step is an interview process that further determines the best placement for the new volunteer. Obviously, a person's talents and interests are key factors in the placement. This interview is a great time to stress the importance of having the volunteer find enjoyment and a sense of worth in what he is doing. It would be a good idea to mention an "open-door policy" and encourage the volunteer to visit with the coordinator if there are any problems or if a particular assignment doesn't seem to be working out.

Adult volunteers are usually trained one-on-one, unless there is a large group beginning at the same time. General items are covered, such as the mission statement and goals of the hospital and particular area they will be working in. The actual job description should be covered in detail and every attempt should be made to eliminate any misunderstandings. The volunteer needs to know exactly what's expected of her. The importance of attendance can also be stressed. Many hospitals expect the volunteer to find a replacement if she is unable to fulfill her assigned time. The specific "hands-on" job training is usually covered with a local resident expert or trainer since these vary greatly.

Supervision of hospital volunteers can vary from little or none to very close supervision in the case of folks on court-ordered community service. Again, open communication or "straight talk" seems to be the most recommended approach. If problems exist, or a volunteer is not happy in what he is doing, it's best to find out about that early on. Reassignment is an easy thing to do, especially if it helps the volunteer feel better about what he is doing.

Since the volunteers are working all over the hospital complex, it is difficult to maintain close contact with them. However, the hospital staff can be encouraged to show their appreciation for the volunteers. A smile and a word of encouragement and support goes a long way in lifting the spirits and making a person feel valued. Periodic meetings in which employees are recognized for their service is a great idea. Of course, the *proper care and feeding* theory suggests that a hospital should at least have an annual volunteer banquet. A free lunch in the hospital cafeteria for volunteers who work a four-hour shift is not unusual. Of course, depending upon the cook, this could be a reward or a punishment. Another suggestion is the recognition of volunteer birthdays with cards or a little something. Sending a get-well card to volunteers who are ill is also a nice touch.

While it is difficult and time-consuming, the coordinator can demonstrate a very caring attitude by making a swing around the hospital once a day. It does so much good to stop, thank the volunteer and ask "How's everything going?" These actions speak loud and clear: *Volunteers are important to us!*

In summary, the hospital world requires very clear goals and expectations for volunteers. Written job descriptions for all volunteer functions are a must and all rules and guidelines should be clearly identified. An "open-door policy" that is alive and well naturally encourages a free and open communication between the volunteer and the coordinator.

Youth Volunteers

Let us now turn our attention to the younger volunteers. Here again, for the sake of space, we will only concentrate on those aspects of volunteer coordination that may be different than working with adults.

The first and probably the most important difference lies in the attention given the volunteer environment, i.e., insuring that it is safe and free of even the slightest hint of sexual abuse. Let's face it – this has been a problem in the church, and we can't pretend it doesn't exist. Even though it may not be as prevalent as the news media would have us believe, we as leaders have a definite responsibility to do everything we can to insure it does not happen in our area of control.

Having said this, there are certain things that church leadership needs to do. The first is to have a published policy stating that *any form of sexual abuse will not be tolerated.* This should be mandated from the highest church levels and reviewed periodically with all staff and volunteers who work with youth. We single out youth because they are obviously the most vulnerable.

On a local level, this policy needs to be printed and formally given to each staff member and volunteer. Legal counsel would recommend that this even needs to be documented with some type of form that the individual reads and signs. This form should include words to the effect that the person acknowledges that he or she has received the policy on sexual misconduct, has read the policy, understands it, and agrees to conduct him- or herself according to the policy. This rather formal approach does two things; first, it demonstrates how important this policy is, and second, it provides the church with the necessary legal documentation to prove it has made a good faith effort to provide an environment free of sexual abuse. Again, this needs to be covered and documented annually.

Now let's look more closely at the young volunteer. For the sake of simplicity we can categorize these folks into two types: those who willingly volunteer, and the "have-to's." The willing helpers are a true joy. You can see the grace of God leading them even at this young age. The secret is to make sure they have a good experience at whatever they do, so that sharing their time becomes something that is natural and grows with their increasing maturity. In many respects, they can be treated as adults because of their motivation.

The "have-to's" are a whole different story. The obvious example of "have to's" are the young people preparing to receive Confirmation. Usually, there are certain *requirements* that they have to complete before reception of the sacrament. As one person commented: "Confirmation is the carrot we dangle in front of them." One element of these is usually some type of service hours.

Many adults who coordinate these programs identify this as the most difficult area of their job. Most young people approach any project like this with a certain amount of fear. Either they have never done volunteer work before and this is a new experience, or they are afraid of the commitment of time. The various lists, contracts and forms can be very intimidating to these novice volunteers. Whatever the case, there is uncertainty and hesitation on their part. Like someone said, "If I had an easy answer to this problem, I could sell it and not have to work for a living!"

In talking to Religious Formation Coordinators, several interesting approaches have surfaced. The first is to pair young volunteers with older teens who can act as mentors and thus insure a good experience for them. This plants the seed in the younger person and keeps the older teen involved in the church while giving a sense of real worth. This side effect for the older teen is one way to combat the "disappearing confirmant." (We never see many of them after Confirmation.)

The second suggestion is to begin volunteer experiences before Confirmation, in fact, as soon as the child begins formal religious formation (even preschool age). This requires planning and coordination on the part of the leader, teacher and parents. It also requires the support and encouragement of the entire church community, including (and beginning with) the clergy.

One innovative idea to encourage parent participation is a sliding scale of costs. The actual cost per child (without any subsidy) is calculated and depending on the level of parent involvement, the cost is adjusted. The more time the parents spend assisting the religious formation program, the cheaper the cost for their child. This seems rather calculated, but it just might work.

One common element in all this is to maintain a combination of work and fun. One leader uses the terms "food, fun and spirituality." Adults often combine fun and food with whatever volunteer work they are involved in. In fact, some churches seem to increase productivity and involvement in direct proportion to the number of potluck dinners they schedule (the "proper feeding"). There has to be some truth to this . . . after all, a study of Scripture reveals our Lord using dinners as a regular setting for His teaching ministry.

The challenges of working with young volunteers seems to require a more creative imagination and willingness to try things for the very first time.

EIGHT

The Best for Last

As the saying goes, we have saved the best for last. Seriously, we can talk about volunteers saving the church immeasurable amounts of money in paid staff. We can write volumes about volunteers developing leadership and deepening fellowship within the church community. We can also revel in the fact that involvement in parish activities leads to ownership which is basic to gospel stewardship. All these things are true and important, but if we fail to see the importance of volunteer spirituality, we have really missed the boat.

If the reason for having church volunteers is simply to "get the job done," we would probably be better off contracting with some temporary employment agency for some warm bodies. When we turn our attention to the spiritual, we face the most important aspect of the whole process of dealing with church volunteers.

In the beautiful economy of salvation, we find that the church cannot make progress toward the kingdom of God without volunteers – and the volunteers find their path to the kingdom of God through their act of volunteering. This is one of those interrelated plans of God that we can't fully understand, so we call it a mystery.

We can accomplish great and wonderful things for the church. We can build buildings, develop programs, stage extravagant religious events; but without a deep spirituality, we are nothing but "a noisy gong, a clanging cymbal" (1 Cor 13:1). St. Augustine is often quoted as saying. "Our hearts are restless until they rest in You." This applies to the volunteer as well as to the church. God, or the spiritual life, is the very foundation of what we do and why we do it.

In the Catechism of the Catholic Church, we find these powerful words: "Since, like all the faithful, lay Christians are entrusted by God with the apostolate by virtue of their Baptism and Confirmation, they have the right and duty, individually or grouped in associations, to work so that the divine message of salvation may be known and accepted by all men throughout the earth. This duty is more pressing when it is only through them that men can hear the Gospel and know Christ. *Their activity* in ecclesial communities *is so necessary that, for the most part, the apostolate of the pastors cannot be fully effective without it"* (paragraph 900, emphasis added).

We also find these words: "The laity can also feel called, or be in fact called, to cooperate with their pastors in the service of the ecclesial community, for the sake of its growth and life. This can be done through the exercise of different kinds of ministries according to the grace and charisms which the Lord has been pleased to bestow on them" (paragraph 910).

Now, we have to be realistic here. We can't expect all lay volunteers to be mini-monks or nuns. That's certainly not the goal. On the other hand, if we completely ignore our responsibility to form and challenge the volunteer to develop spiritual life, we just might have a serious accounting to make to our Lord. By our baptism, we are all called to become saints. We have been given a special responsibility in this arena because we find ourselves entrusted with our group of volunteers.

Francis de Sales, besides being a saint, was a very practical man. In his book *Introduction to the Devout Life,* he wrote that "the practice of devotion must be adapted to the strength, to the occupation and to the duties of each one in particular."

When we plan meeting agendas that include prayer, reflection and sharing, we can put this advice to good use. Any opportunities for spiritual growth must take into account the group as a whole and where each individual is in his or her faith journey.

Now, here are just a few practical things we can do to foster this growth in the spiritual life:

1. Begin in the training. This means that as the volunteer receives the special training for that particular ministry or organization, the spiritual aspects of what they are doing are discussed. This shouldn't be an "add on" or supplement to the training – this should be integrated into the heart of the training. We should be

this as the very foundation of who the group is and the work it does. This gives us our identity!

2. Periodic meetings can be an effective tool and spirituality can play an important part in the agenda. Just one example is the St. Vincent de Paul Society. This group has weekly meetings and a regular part of each agenda is devoted to prayer and study.

3. Some groups have found that reading the Sunday's Gospel, followed by reflection and faith sharing is far more beneficial to spiritual growth than the customary Our Father said in haste at the beginning of a meeting. Attachment 6 is an example of a prayer service that can be used for almost any group of volunteers that meet. These prayer aids can be as formal as this prepared sheet, or they can be as simple as reading the next Sunday's Gospel and asking each one in the group to share what touched him or her about the text. The Serendipity New Testament is an excellent tool for such discussion questions. There are any number of sources available to facilitate this type of faith sharing. Your local religious bookstores can help you find one that should work for your group. Keep in mind that if the group has never done any faith sharing, the first few times may be a little uncomfortable, but patience and perseverance pays off.

4. Another suggestion is to have periodic events that focus on the spirituality of the group. Days of recollection, group retreats, participation in parish missions or "in-service evenings" are just a few examples. When we had our parish mission, we asked the leader to hold a special session for the ministry/organization heads. This leadership session focused on their special call and what specific virtues they as parish leaders would find most helpful.

    The Pastor and staff are excellent resources for these events. Some dioceses have people on the staff who are trained in leading these sessions. Oftentimes, the Deacon community can be a great resource to also keep in mind.

    Attachment 7 is an example of a Retreat Day for for Catechists. Something like this can be easily modified to fit your individual needs.

5. One other resource that I have found helpful when preparing agendas for prayer services is a collection of various quotations

dealing with ministry. Attachment 8 is just a few of these that are taken from Scripture, some from the writings of the Saints and others from church documents. Here again, many other resources are available and your local religious bookstore can be a great help in searching for these.

When all is said and done, we can recruit, train and supervise volunteers like "super managers." All the jobs can be completed to perfection and completed on time. However, if we fail to challenge the spiritual growth of each person in the group, we are failing to live up to the calling each one of us received when we accepted our assignment as leaders. We are also failing those we lead.

Registration Form

PLEASE PRINT

Family Information

Last Name_____ Phone_____

Address_____ City _____

Zip_____

Marital Status: Married___ Single___ Divorced___ Widowed___

Date of Marriage ___/___/___ Place_____,___ (City, State)

Is your marriage recognized by the Catholic Church? Yes___ No___

Uncertain___

First Names: Male_____ Female_____

Date of Birth ___/___/___ Date of Birth ___/___/___

Maiden Name _____

Sacraments

Please check: Baptism   _____   Baptism   _____

First Communion _____   First Communion _____

Confirmation   _____   Confirmation   _____

Education (Please fill in name and location.)

Grade School _____ _____

High School _____ _____

Graduate   (Y or N)   (Y or N)

College _____ _____

Graduate   (Y or N)   (Y or N)

Highest Degree_____ _____

Profession/Trade _____ _____

Employer (or former)_____ _____

Work Phone _____ _____

Religion (Active Y or N)_____ (Active Y or N)_____

If not Catholic, name of church attending _____

Children living at home

	Oldest Child	Second Child	Third Child
Name	_____	_____	_____
D.O.B.	__/__/__	__/__/__	__/__/__

Sacraments (Please circle Y or N.)

Baptism	Y or N	Y or N	Y or N
First Communion	Y or N	Y or N	Y or N
Confirmation	Y or N	Y or N	Y or N

Education (Please fill in name.)

Grade School	_____	_____	_____
High School	_____	_____	_____
College	_____	_____	_____

Children living at home

	Fourth Child	Fifth Child	Sixth Child
Name	_____	_____	_____
D.O.B.	__/__/__	__/__/__	__/__/__

Sacraments (Please circle Y or N.)

Baptism	Y or N	Y or N	Y or N
First Communion	Y or N	Y or N	Y or N
Confirmation	Y or N	Y or N	Y or N

Education (Please fill in name.)

Grade School	_____	_____	_____
High School	_____	_____	_____
College	_____	_____	_____

****

Emergency Contact _____

Address_____ Phone_____

Have you been in this parish before? (Y or N)

If yes, when were you last registered? __/__/__

For Office Use
Date Received __/__/__by Telepone___ by Mail___ Collection___
Envelope No._____
Data Base Updated __/__/__ by (name)_____
Envelope Co. Updated __/__/__ by (name)_____
Welcome Letter Sent __/__/__ by (name)_____
Home Visit by Welcomers__/__/__ by_____

OPPORTUNITIES TO BECOME INVOLVED

Holy Ghost parish stresses the importance of stewardship as a way of life to help all parishioners increase their faith experience. Listed below are the ministries and organizations we have in the parish. Please check your interests.

Ministries	Male	Female	Child (Name)
Altar Servers	____	____	_____
Eucharistic Ministers	____	____	_____
Family Life	____	____	_____
Funeral Network	____	____	_____
H.O.P.E. (Widows group)	____	____	_____
Liturgy Committee	____	____	_____
Lectors	____	____	_____
Music/Choir	____	____	_____
Men's Prayer Group	____	____	_____
Prayer Chain	____	____	_____
Religious Ed. (Teacher)	____	____	_____
Stewardship	____	____	_____
St. Vincent de Paul	____	____	_____
Sunday Preschool	____	____	_____

Organizations			
Golden Age Group	____	____	_____
Hospitality Committee	____	____	_____
June Jamboree	____	____	_____
Men's Club	____	____	_____
Money Counters	____	____	_____
Parent-Teacher Org.	____	____	_____
Parish Council	____	____	_____
School Board	____	____	_____
School Volunteers	____	____	_____
Ushers	____	____	_____
Women's Group	____	____	_____

Calling Script

Hello_____. This is_____ I'm a fellow parishioner at _____ Parish. We are conducting a brief survey of parishioners to determine if the parish is reaching the needs of its members. Would you have just a few minutes to answer some questions and give us your opinion on a few issues?

(If not)
   What would be a good time to call back? _____

(if now is a good time)
   1. What do you feel are some of the parish's strengths?
   2. What do you feel are some of the parish's weaknesses?
   3. Are you currently active in any of the parish ministries or organizations?

(if not active)
   Could you explain why?

(if active)
   4. Were you active in your previous parish or church?
   5. Is there anything the parish could do to make it easier for you to be more involved?
   6. Is there any support you would like to see the parish provide that is not currently available?

THANK YOU_____! I appreciate the time you spent answering these questions. Your thoughts and opinions will be very helpful in directing the activities and services of the parish in the future.

BYE NOW.

Attachment 3

Invitation Letter

Dear _____,

Have you ever gone to an amusement park or a county fair and just walked around looking at the rides, games, and food concessions without actually taking part in the fun? You could probably say you were a "spectator" and not a "participant."

We have so many activities, ministries and organizations in our parish that it's a little like a fair – so much to choose from.

If your participation has been limited to Sunday worship only, we would encourage you to consider taking that first step and becoming involved in just one of the many groups in the parish.

You may want to take a little time to study the various activities and see if there is one organization or group that appeals to you more than others. If your interests are in an area that we don't currently have, we need to know that also. This is how new groups are formed.

Many studies have proven that people who participate in activities outside the regular worship service feel more connected to the community and enjoy a greater sense of "belonging."

The group you join is in need of your talents. Each person has something of value to share, and the whole group suffers loss when you aren't a part of it.

Maybe you've never thought about joining in this way before. Well, now's your chance. Again, we encourage you to give serious consideration to making the switch from "spectator" to "participant." This is how each of us can help the kingdom of God grow right before our eyes.

Sincerely,

[You may want to consider including a list of all the parish ministries/organizations with the coordinators' names and phone numbers.]

Attachment 4

Commissioning Ceremony for Evangelization Committee

Song

"Like a Shepherd" by Bob Dufford, S.J. (Use your local song booklet.)

Opening Prayer

Leader: My brothers and sisters, we are gathered here to respond to God's invitation to our common ministry of reconciliation. Open your hearts to the Lord.

All: We will praise God's holy name.

Scripture

Read Ezekiel 34:11-16.
Moment of silence

Response

All: Lord, send out your Spirit.

Leader: The spirit of the Lord
will be poured upon us;
then shall the desert
become fertile land.

All: Lord, send out your Spirit.

Leader: The spirit of God moves us to bring
good news to the poor and the stranger,
to the blind, new vision,
to prisoners, freedom.

All: Lord, send out your Spirit.

Leader: Yes, as the earth nurtures its crops
          that all might share,
          so will our God bring to birth
          the Spirit within us.

All: Lord, send out your Spirit.

Homily
(Brief comments pointing out that God is calling these volunteers to work in the area of evangelization, to share his special ministry and that they will receive His special help in their work.)

Commissioning Rite
(While each person comes forward, the group sings Ubi Caritas.*)*

(Name) _____, do you accept the call from the Lord to walk as a sponsor with those on the road to reconciliation with the Lord and the Church?

Sponsor: I do !

(The leader makes the sign of the cross with oil on the forehead of the person.)

(Name) _____, accept this oil (you can also use holy water) as a sign of God's love for you, which you are called to share in this ministry of reconciliation.

Sponsor: "The Spirit of the Lord is upon me because the Lord
          has anointed me. He has sent me to bring glad tidings
          to the lowly, to proclaim liberty to the captives."

(After all have received the anointing.)

Leader: Let us pray.

O Lord, you have called us to share in the healing ministry of your son Jesus Christ. Strengthened by the example of the Good Shepherd and blessed with this holy oil, may we serve your people with compassion and love. We ask this in the name of our brother Jesus.

All: Amen!

Sing the blessing:

May the peace of the Lord be with you.
With your friends and your family, too.
Let it be and let it grow, and everywhere you go.
May the peace of the Lord follow you.

Attachment 5

Rite of Blessing for Catechists[1]

The homily follows the Gospel reading. In it the celebrant, basing himself on the sacred text, gives an explanation of the celebration pertinent to the particular place and the people involved.

Following the homily, the celebrant, deacon, or other suitable minister calls the catechists to come forward. They may be called individually by name or as a group.

The celebrant may then introduce the blessing, using the following, or similar words:

> For the pastoral activity of the church, the cooperation of a great many people is needed, so that communities as well as individuals may advance to full maturity in faith through the celebration of the liturgy, through study, and through their manner of life.
>
> This cooperation is provided by those who devote themselves to catechesis. Enlightened by God's word and the teaching of the Church, catechists impart to others an initiation or a deeper foundation in those realities that they themselves have learned as truths to be followed in living and to be celebrated in liturgy.
>
> In this celebration, we will bless the name of the Lord for giving us such coworkers, and pray that through the Holy Spirit they will receive the grace they need in their service to the Church.

When someone is being admitted to the catechetical ministry for the first time, it may be appropriate for them to express their willingness to exercise this ministry before the liturgical assembly. In such cases, the priest may add the following:

> God the Father, Son, and Holy Spirit has called us to be wise stewards of the Good News. This requires conviction, hope, enthusiasm, and love.

---

1. Taken from *Image God's Mercy*, Catechetical Sunday 1995 Copyright© 1995 United States Catholic Conference, Washington, D.C. 20017. Used with permission.

Now I ask you, (name of catechist), are you willing to exercise the ministry of catechesis as (name of level) in (name of parish)?

Catechist:
With the assistance of God's grace, I am ready and willing to serve as a catechist. May I, along with all the catechists of this parish, be a good steward of what God has entrusted to me.

Deacon or minister:
We ask the community to signify its support and acceptance of your commitment with applause.

General Intercessions

The general intercessions follow, either in the form usual at Mass or in the form given here. The celebrant concludes the general intercessions with the prayer of blessing.

Celebrant:
Since God wills the salvation of all, let us pray to him in these words:

R: Lord, draw all people to yourself.
Or:
R: Lord, hear our prayer.

Assisting minister:
Father, grant that all people will come to know you, the one true God, and Jesus Christ, whom you have sent. (For this we pray:) R.

Send workers into your harvest, so that your name will be glorified among the nations. (For this we pray:) R.

You sent the disciples of Jesus to preach the Gospel; help us to spread the victory of his cross. (For this we pray:) R.

Make us docile to the teaching of the apostles and our lives consistent with the truths we believe. (For this we pray:) R.

As you call us to serve you in our brothers and sisters, make us the ministers of your truth. (For this we pray:) R.

Keep us as faithful ministers of your Church, so that, having taught others, we ourselves may be found faithful in your service. (For this we pray:) R.

May the grace of the Holy Spirit guide our hearts and our lips, so that we may remain constant in loving and praising you. (For this we pray:) R.

Prayer of Blessing

With hands outstretched, the celebrant says the prayer of blessing:

With your fatherly blessing, Lord, strengthen these servants of yours in their resolve to dedicate themselves as catechists. Grant that they will strive to share with others what they themselves derive from pondering your word and studying the Church's teaching. And let them gladly join those they teach in honoring and serving your name.

We ask this through Christ our Lord.

R. Amen.

As an alternative, if this seems more opportune, the prayer of blessing may be used at the end of Mass after the following or some other invitation.

Bow your heads and pray for God's blessing.

After the prayer of blessing, each catechist may be presented with a Bible, the catechism of the Catholic Church, and/or a certificate. If it has not already taken place and is desirable, the congregation may signify its support by applause, and acclamation, or an appropriate hymn.

Prayer Service

Instructions

- Please read the Scripture reading and the introduction and the questions that follow.

- Then have the people count off and form groups of three or four each.

- Give them three minutes to think about their responses to the questions.

- Give them five minutes to share their answers within their small groups. (You might warn them that with this short time limit, each person will have only about one or two minutes to share his or her answers.)

LEADER: The Scripture reading for today is from Luke 24:13-32.

Two of the disciples of Jesus that same day were making their way to a village named Emmaus seven miles distant from Jerusalem, discussing as they went all that had happened. In the course of their lively exchange, Jesus approached and began to walk along with them. However, they were restrained from recognizing him. He said to them, "What are you discussing as you go your way?" They halted in distress, and one of them, Cleopas by name, asked him, "Are you the only resident of Jerusalem who does not know the things that went on there these past few days?" . . . Then he said to them, "What little sense you have! How slow you are to believe all that the prophets have announced! Did not the Messiah have to undergo all this so as to enter into his glory?" Beginning, then, with Moses and all the prophets, he interpreted for them every passage of Scripture which referred to him. By now they were near the village to which they were going, and he acted as if he were going farther. But they pressed him: "Stay

with us. It is nearly evening . . . When he had seated himself
with them to eat, he took bread, pronounced the blessing,
and then broke the bread and began to distribute it to them.
With that their eyes were opened and they recognized him;
whereupon he vanished from their sight.

LEADER: Take a moment and think about your answers to these questions:

1. Have you ever felt like running away or throwing in the towel
   spiritually?

2. What is the thing that triggers a spiritual crisis in your experience?

3. What helps you recognize Jesus walking alongside you when you
   are down spiritually?

Retreat Day for Catechists[1]

Preparation

One parish or several parishes could sponsor the retreat day (9 a.m. to 4 p.m.). Invite all those involved in catechetical ministry. Encourage preregistration.

Location: Select the most comfortable, cheerful space available. Supplies to have on hand; round tables with glasses and pitchers of ice water, hot/cold beverages, and pastries. Also, ask hospitality greeters to welcome people and answer questions.

Decorations: Catechetical 1995 posters and symbols; live plants; posters or banners listing the spiritual and corporal works of mercy; and Scripture quotations that show God's everlasting mercy, such as Psalm 118:1-2, "Give thanks to the Lord for he is good, for his mercy endures forever," or Matthew 5:8, "Blessed are the merciful for they shall obtain mercy."

Assignment: Encourage prospective attendees to clip a newspaper article demonstrating mercy by an individual and to bring it with them to the retreat. Ask them to bring their Bibles.

Retreat Schedule

9:00 Arrival and getting settled at the round tables.

9:30 Facilitator's greeting: The purpose of this retreat is to provide an opportunity to reflect on God's mercy in your life and to strengthen your partnership with Christ in being merciful to others.
Prayer: Colossians 3:12-17 or Catechist's Prayer from Catechetical Booklet.
Song: "By Name I Have Called You."

---

1. Taken from *Image God's Mercy*, Catechetical Sunday 1995 Copyright© 1995 United States Catholic Conference, Washington, D.C. 20017. Used with permission

10:00   Ask for five volunteers to talk briefly about their article and why they chose it. Under the heading "Concepts of Mercy," have someone record descriptive words on newsprint to see what the group's understanding of the meaning of mercy is. It may include compassion, care, kindness, justice, tenderness, forgiveness, love, and understanding.

11:00   Break

11:15   Ask participants to listen quietly to the presentation and recall times when the healing mercy of God was given to them. Then have them examine their own actions in the last month to see when opportunities calling for mercy arose and how they reacted. Encourage everyone to thank God for the power to be merciful, and recognizing their dependence, to ask for God's forgiveness for those times that they failed.

Possible points to incorporate in the presentation:

- The word *mercy* is found in both Testaments but retains all the primitive value of the Hebrew word *hesed*, which indicates love more than pity (New American Bible, p. 338).

- Mercy is often communal. We give and receive; give generously, receive abundantly. The need of the broken person puts us in touch with our own brokenness; it becomes mutually healing.

- The prologue of the Rule of Benedict says, "Listen, and attend with the ear of your heart." Listen involves becoming aware of another's pain. It means clearing away our preoccupation with ourselves.

- Superficiality is a problem for all of us. Outwardly, we may seem concerned but if we do not love, it's do-gooder action. Without love we cannot be truly merciful.

- Understanding mercy is of value only when you incorporate it in your behavior.

12:00   Break for lunch

Afternoon

1:00   Reassembling song: "Here I am Lord." Table storytelling follows. Ask participants to reread or recall the parable of the prodigal son. Luke 15:11-32. Encourage participants to think of a time in their life when they were one of three people; the prodigal son, the older son who stayed home, or the father. Allow a few moments for participants to collect their thoughts in order to tell their story to the table group. Questions include the following: What happened and how did you feel about about it? Were compassion, justice and forgiveness evident? What did you learn from this experience?

1:30   Assign to each table a spiritual and corporal work of mercy and two newsprint sheets. Tell each table group to discuss how they as individuals and as Christian ministers respond to the cries of need of the two assigned works of mercy. Is change necessary to bring about a merciful response? If so, where and how in the world, the Church, the parish, the individual? List some "Roadblocks to Acts of Mercy." Record on the newsprint the chief points of the discussion.

2:00   Tape newsprint sheets to walls. Then invite the large group to discuss the challenges posted.

2:45   Reflection time: Pray, meditate and reflect on the day. First, with two helpers, summarize how the works of mercy challenge us and how the call to mercy came up during the day. Next, ask five volunteers to prepare a prayer bringing into focus the partnership with Christ in being merciful.

3:15   Give a summary that has been recorded on newsprint in advance for the group to copy. (Remove all other newsprint.) Group questions or comments.

3:40   Prayer of partnership with Christ.
Response: "Give thanks to the Lord for he is good, for his mercy endures forever" (Ps. 118:1-2).
Final song: "City of God"

Selected Quotations

Scripture:

"Thanks be to God, who unfailingly leads us on in Christ's triumphal train, and employs us to diffuse the fragrance of his knowledge everywhere!" (2 Corinthians 2:14)

This one is great when we meet with difficulties: ". . . in all that we do we strive to present ourselves as ministers of God, acting with patient endurance amid trials, difficulties, beatings, imprisonments, and riots; as men familiar with hard work, sleepless nights, and fastings; conducting ourselves with innocence, knowledge, and patience, in the Holy Spirit, in sincere love as men with the message of truth and the power of God; wielding the weapons of righteousness with right hand and left, whether honored or dishonored, spoken of well or ill. We are called impostors, yet we are truthful; nobodies who are in fact well known; dead, yet here we are alive; punished, but not put to death, sorrowful, though we are always rejoicing; poor, yet we enrich many. We seem to have nothing, yet everything is ours!" (2 Corinthians 6:4-10)

This is excellent to show to various talents and gifts: "Just as each of us has one body with many members, and not all the members have the same function, so too we, though many, are one body in Christ and individually members one of another. We have gifts that differ according to the favor bestowed on each of us. . . . It may be the gift of ministry; it should be used for service. . . ." (Romans 12:4-19)

This section shows that God is the one really working through us: "I planted the seed and Apollos watered it, but God made it grow. This means that neither he who plants nor he who waters is of any special account, only God, who gives the growth. He who plants and he who waters work to the same end. Each will receive his wages in proportion to his toil. We are God's co-workers, while you are his cultivation, his building." (1 Corinthians 3:6-9)

"Although I am not bound to anyone, I made myself the slave of all so as to win over as many as possible. . . . I have made myself all things to all men in order to save at least some of them. In fact, I do all that I do for the sake of the Gospel in the hope of having a share in its blessings." (1 Corinthians 9:19-23)

"What I do is discipline my own body and master it, for fear that after having preached to others I myself should be rejected." (1 Corinthians 9:27)

This is an excellent example of our Lord delegating his authority. Notice that he also gave them the necessary training: "Jesus summoned the Twelve and began to send them out two by two, giving them authority over unclean spirits. He instructed them to take nothing on the journey but a walking stick. . . ." (Mark 6:7-10)

Here is just one example of our Lord giving positive reinforcement to those he came in contact with: ". . . Then Jesus said in reply, 'Woman, you have great faith! Your wish will come to pass.' That very moment her daughter got better." (Matthew 15:28)

This is an example of Jesus asking his apostles for feedback: "One day when Jesus was praying in seclusion and his disciples were with him, he put the question to them, "Who do the crowds say that I am?" (Luke 9:18-19) You can also see a similar report in Mark 8:27.

This is a beautiful example of clear instructions being given by our Lord: ". . . He sent two of his disciples with these instructions: 'Go into the city and you will come upon a man carrying a water jar. Follow him. Whatever house he enters, say to the owner, 'The Teacher asks, Where is my guest room where I may eat the Passover with my disciples?' Then he will show you an upstairs room, spacious, furnished, and all in order. That is the place you are to get ready for us . . ." (Mark 14:13-16)

The necessity of prayer can be seen in the many examples our Lord gave us. Here is just one. "He often retired to deserted places and prayed." (Luke 5:16)

Other Sources

The following quotation from Adrian Van Kaam is from his book *Spirituality and the Gentle Life* (1974). He is commenting on how our selfishness can hinder our ministry. "They prevent me from becoming an attractive sign and radiant incarnation of divine gentleness and love."

The *Catechism of the Catholic Church* is an excellent source for ministry in the church. Paragraphs 900 and 910 were quoted earlier and are just a few examples.

The *Imitation of Christ* by Thomas à Kempis is an excellent source for ideas on ministries. (Be sure to use a newer translation.) The following chapters are particularly helpful:

15 "Of Works Done out of Charity"

22 "Of the Consideration of Human Misery"

38 "Of the Good Government of Ourselves in Outward Things, and of Having Recourse to God in Dangers"

39 "That a Man Must Not Be Too Anxious about His Affairs."

41 "Of the Contempt of All Temporal Honors."

The Encyclical *Lumen Gentium* is also a wonderful resource in this area as well as the Decree on the Apostolate of Lay People (*Apostolicam Actuositatem*).